Gorilla

Tiger

Giraffe

Spotted Cuscus

Old World Vulture

Bison

Orangutan

Elk

Proboscis Monkey

1

WILDLIFE OUR PRIDE

THE BOOK OF PRIMATES

By

Nazil Abbas

VOLUME 1

Copyright

Bobcat
Gorilla
Honey Badger
Panther
Elephant
Harpy Eagle
Spotted Hyena
Kudu
Cheetah

TABLE OF CONTENTS

DEDICATION

This book is foremost dedicated to God almighty and to the entire wildlife conservators.

ACKNOWLEDGEMENT

All gratitude belong to God Almighty the alpha and the Omega, the omniscient, omnipotent and omnipresent for allowing this project to see the light of the day.

My profound gratitude goes to my family and friends for their support during the course of researching for the finding of this wonderful project.

Posterity won't forgive me if I forget to acknowledge you, our great scholar and teacher of our century **Mualim Swolahuddeen Uthman** May Almighty God forgive all your shortcomings and grant you heaven above all. Amen!

To all my clue members I appreciate all your supports for this wonderful project to see the light of the day, from my heart I do appreciate!

INTRODUCTION

The actions of humans have created many threats to wild animals and wildlife in general. As human populations increase, these threats multiply, leading to a fewer number of some species, and total extinction of others. All animals contribute to the ecology of the earth and are vital to its health and continuation.

Many wildlife species are threatened with extinction, and many critical wildlife habitats are being destroyed. The need for conservation was created by human beings. The problems are large and complex requiring the combined efforts and cooperation of numerous groups, organizations, local people and agencies around the world. But most importantly, preservation and protection of wildlife and their habitats starts with each individual human.

Together, we all play an important role in protecting wild animals, wildlife in general and their homes. By joining a conservation organization, welcoming wildlife into your yard with native plants, reducing and recycling, refraining from using of herbicides and pesticides, and speaking out for wildlife and nature, you can help wild animals everyday.

MAMMALIANS

Mammals are animals that have warm-blood, fur or hair and usually have live babies. A few mammals lay eggs rather than giving birth to live babies, including the platypus and the spiny anteater. All mammals have some type of body hair or fur, though marine mammals, like dolphins and whales, are almost hairless. Over 5,500 species of mammals have been recorded to date, compared to more than 28,000 species of fish and over 1,000,000 species of insects.

Many mammal babies are helpless when first born, but a few species, including Zebras and Moose, can walk from the day they are born. Marsupial babies, like Kangaroos and Opossum, are born as small as a pinkie nail and move to their mother's pouch to mature. All mammal babies drink milk from their mothers.

Mammals maintain their body temperatures to just about the same temperature all the time, despite the temperature outside their bodies. Warm blood allows mammals to be very active and live in a wide variety of environments. Fur and fat help protect mammals in the cold, while sweating or panting releases extra heat for mammals in hot conditions.

PRIMATES

Primate, in zoology, any mammal of the group that includes the lemurs, lorises, tarsiers, monkeys, apes, and humans. The order Primates, including more than 500 species, is the third most diverse order of mammals, after rodents (Rodentia) and bats (Chiroptera).

Although there are some notable variations between some primate groups, they share several anatomic and functional characteristics reflective of their common ancestry. When compared with body weight, the primate brain is larger than that of other terrestrial mammals, and it has a fissure unique to primates (*Calcarine sulcus*) that separates the first and second visual areas on each side of the brain. Whereas all other mammals have claws or hooves on their digits, only primates have flat nails. Some primates do have claws, but even among these, there is a flat nail on the big toe (hallux). In all primates except humans, the hallux diverges from the other toes and together with them forms a pincer capable of grasping objects such as branches. Not all primates have similarly dextrous hands; only the catarrhines (Old World monkeys, apes, and humans) and a few of the lemurs and lorises have an opposable thumb.

Primates are not alone in having grasping feet, but as these occur in many other arboreal mammals (e.g., squirrels and opossums), and as most present-day primates are arboreal, this characteristic suggests that they evolved from an ancestor that was arboreal. So too does primates' possession of specialized nerve endings (Meissner's corpuscles) in the hands and feet that increase tactile sensitivity. As far as is known, no other placental mammal has them. Primates possess dermatoglyphics (the skin ridges responsible for fingerprints), but so do many other arboreal mammals.

The eyes face forward in all primates so that the eyes' visual fields overlap. Again, this feature is not by any means restricted to primates, but it is a general feature seen among predators. It has been proposed, therefore, that the ancestor of the primates was a predator, perhaps insectivorous. The optic fibres in almost all mammals cross over (decussate) so that signals from one eye are interpreted on the opposite side of the brain, but, in some primate species, up to 40 percent of the nerve fibres do not cross over.

MONKEY

Monkeys are found in two main regions of the world, so scientists have grouped them as either Old World monkeys or New World monkeys. Old World monkeys are found in Africa and Asia. Some examples are guenons, mangabeys, macaques, baboons, and colobus monkeys. New World monkeys are found in Mexico, Central America, and South America. Some examples are woolly monkeys, spider monkeys, howler monkeys, capuchin monkeys, and squirrel monkeys. Marmosets and tamarins also live in New World habitats but are different enough to be in their own different scientific grouping.

There are a few characteristics that are different in Old World and New World monkeys:

> Noses: Most Old World monkeys have small curved nostrils set close together. Most New World monkeys have round nostrils set far apart.

> Cheek pouches: Macaques and some of the other Old World monkeys have cheek pouches, where food is stuffed on the run, so it can be chewed later. New World monkeys

don't have cheek pouches.

➢ Rump pads: Some Old World monkeys, such as drills, have sitting pads on their rumps, but New World monkeys do not.

➢ Tails: Some New World monkeys, such as spider monkeys, have prehensile tails, but Old World monkeys do not. And one Old World monkey, the Barbary macaque, has no tail at all!

Wolf's Mona Monkey
Golden Monkey
Javan Langur
Proboscis Monkey
Olive Baboon
Red-shanked Douc
SILVERED LEAF MONKEY
Lion-Tailed Monkey
Red Face Ateles

PROBOSCIS MONKEY

The Proboscis monkey is an Old World monkey with a characteristic long nose that distinguishes this animal from other monkeys. As a matter of fact, another name of this primate is 'Monyet belanda' monkey, literally meaning 'long-nosed' monkey. When first seeing this animal, people didn't suppose it was a monkey because of its rather unusual appearance. Thus, males of this species exhibit extremely long noses of up to 7 inches, which are likely to attract females whose noses are usually shorter. Another important characteristic of Proboscis monkeys is their diverse color patterns, varying from bright orange to yellow or pink. Additionally, newborn Proboscis monkey display blue faces that turn to cream color as they grow up.

SCIENTIFIC CLASSIFICATION

Kingdom:	Animalia
Phylum:	Chordata
Class:	Mammalia
Order:	Primates
Family:	Cercopithecidae
Genus:	Nasalis
Species:	N. larvatus
Binomial name:	*Nasalis larvatus*

FACT ABOUT PROBOSCIS MONKEY

- ✓ Mating Behavior: Polygyny
- ✓ Reproduction: February-November
- ✓ Pregnancy Duration: 166 Days
- ✓ Baby Carrying: 1 Infant
- ✓ Independent Age: 1 Year
- ✓ Female Name: Female
- ✓ Male Name: Male
- ✓ Baby Name: Infant
- ✓ Sexual Maturity: 4years
- ✓ Group Name: Troop, Band, Harem
- ✓ Lifestyle: Arboreal, Altricial, Island Endemic, Viviparous

MATING HABITS

Proboscis monkeys have a polygynous mating system, where the dominant male mates with females in a troop. They breed between February and November. The gestation period lasts for 166 days, yielding one infant, typically during the nighttime hours. The newborn baby exhibits a deep blue face and sparse, almost black coat, which changes its color within 3-4 months after birth. Collective rearing is common in this species: females of a troop help raise each other's offspring. They can also suckle another female's young when needed. During the first year of its life, the infant is constantly with its mother. However, soon the female produces another baby, after which young females usually continue living with their natal group, whereas males disperse, joining all-male bachelor groups. The age of reproductive maturity is 4 years old in females and 4-5 years old in males.

DIET AND NUTRITION

Being herbivorous (folivorous and frugivorous) creatures, these primates generally feed upon fruits, seeds, young leaves, and shoots of mangroves, supplementing this diet with occasional caterpillars, larvae, and other invertebrates.

HABITS AND LIFESTYLE

Proboscis monkeys are highly social animals, forming troops of 2-30 animals, typically consisting of a single dominant male and multiple (up to 10) females with their offspring. Males defend their group by exposing their teeth and emitting loud, honking signals, while females are responsible for foraging and caring for infants. In areas with sufficient food or close to the water, these troops may occasionally unite in larger aggregations. During these times, groups of Proboscis monkeys rest and sleep among mangroves at the edge of the water. The presence of freshwater bodies such as swamps or rivers is the primary life condition for these animals. Proboscis monkeys are accomplished swimmers. Moreover, when foraging or fleeing from a threat, they are able to take deep dives. Proboscis monkeys communicate with each other using various vocalizations. When claiming the status of the group, males will emit honks; they will also produce alarm calls to signal danger. Both sexes give threat calls, but each are different. In addition, females and immature individuals will emit so-called "female calls" when angry. These monkeys will also make honks, roars, and snarls. Nonvocal displays include leaping-branch shaking, and bare-teeth open mouth threats.

DISTRIBUTION AND GEOGRAPHY

- ✓ Continents: Asia

- ✓ Subcontinents: Southeast Asia

- ✓ Countries: Brunei, Indonesia, Malaysia

- ✓ Biomes: Mangrove, Tropical Moist Forests

These animals are native and endemic exclusively to the island of Borneo in southeastern Asia, where they generally live in coastal areas, covered with mangroves and swamp forests. Other suitable habitats include lowlands along rivers as well as riparian forests and rainforests. Proboscis monkeys typically live in close proximity to water bodies of their home range.

BASIC FACT ABOUT PROBOSCIS MONKEY

- ✓ Life Span: 13-23 Years

- ✓ Top Speed: 24 Km/H

- ✓ Weight: 7-22.5 Kg

- ✓ Length: 53-76 Cm

POPULATION THREATS

Currently, the biggest threat to this species is the loss of their natural habitat as a result of forest fires and the cutting of mangrove trees, growing along riverbanks. Meanwhile, those in coastal areas lose their range due to the development of human settlements and shrimp farms. Another serious concern is localized hunting for food and intestinal bezoar stones, used in traditional medicine. This threat is compounded by the docile nature of these animals, making them 'easy prey' for hunters.

SILVERED LEAF MONKEY

Silvered leaf monkey or Silvery langur are medium-sized Old World monkeys with a long, non-prehensile tail. They have grey-tipped, dark brown or black fur, giving the animals a uniform silvery appearance. Unlike some related species, there are no paler markings on the face or body, except for a patch of whitish hair on the groin of females. A crest of fur runs along the top of the head, and the hair on the cheeks is long, often obscuring the ears. The hands and feet are hairless, with dark-colored skin, and have opposable thumbs and toes.

SCIENTIFIC CLASSIFICATION

Kingdom: Animalia

Phylum: Chordata

Class: Mammalia

Order: Primates

Family: Cercopithecidae

Genus: Trachypithecus

Species: T. cristatus

Binomial Name: *Trachypithecus cristatus*

FACT ABOUT SILVERED LEAF MONKEY

- ✓ Mating Behavior: Polygyny
- ✓ Reproduction Season: Year-Round
- ✓ Gestation: 181-200 Days
- ✓ Baby Carrying: 1 Infant
- ✓ Independent Age: 18 Months
- ✓ Female Name: Female
- ✓ Male Name: Male
- ✓ Baby Name: Infant

MATING HABITS

Silvery lutungs are polygynous whic means that one male mates with more than one females during the breeding season. The female attracts the male by making side-to-side motions with her head. Silvery lutungs breed year round, with no clear breeding season, although each female typically gives birth once every 18-24 months. Females give birth to a single infant after a gestation period of 181-200 days. The young weigh about 400 grams (14 oz) and are well developed, with a strong grip for holding onto the mother. Infants are born with orange fur, and with white hairless skin on the face, hands, and feet. The skin rapidly changes to the dark adult colour, but the fur does not reach the adult pattern for 3-5 months after birth. The young are cared for by females communally, and are not weaned for 18 months, even though the biological mother stops lactating after just 12 months. The young become reproductively mature almost as soon as they finish weaning, and, on average, females first give birth at 35 months of age.

BASIC FACT ABOUT SILVERED LEAF MONKEY

- ✓ Life Span: 31 Years

- ✓ Weight: 5.7 - 6.6 Kg

- ✓ Length: 46 - 58 Cm

- ✓ Group Name: Troop, Barrel, Cartload, Tribe, Wilderness.

- ✓ Lifestyle: Arboreal, Precocial, Browsing, Nomadic, Scansorial, Terrestrial, Territorial.

DISTRIBUTION AND GEOGRAPHY

- ✓ Continents: Asia
- ✓ Subcontinents: Southeast Asia
- ✓ Countries: Brunei, Indonesia, Malaysia
- ✓ Biomes: Mangrove, Tropical Moist Forests

HABITATS

Silvery lutungs are found across Borneo and Sumatra, as well as in parts of the south-western Malay peninsula, the Natuna Islands, and other nearby islands. These monkeys live in mangrove swamps and nearby forest regions, and usually avoid travelling far from coasts or rivers.

HABITS AND LIFESTYLE

Silvery lutungs are diurnal and travel in groups of around 9-40 individuals with one adult male and many adult females communally caring for infants. They rarely leave the trees, which provide them protection from ground-dwelling predators, and rapidly flee if threatened. During the day, these monkeys may travel up to 500 metres (1,600 ft) through the forest and at night then the entire group will shelter in a single tree. The social structure of silvery lutungs is matrilineal and harem based. Females remain in the group for life, while males leave shortly after reaching adulthood. Within the group, males dominate the females, and females with young dominate those without. In order to communicate with each other Silvery lutungs make at least thirteen different vocalizations, with the most common being used by adult males defending their territory. Other vocalizations express fear, anger, excitement, and satisfaction, in addition to various calls made by infants.

DIET AND NUTRITION

Silvery lutungs are DIET Herbivore, Folivore; herbivores (foliovres) feeding mainly on leaves. Their diet also includes fruit, and some seeds and flowers.

POPULATION NUMBER

The IUCN Red List and other sources don't provide the number of the Silvery lutung total population size. Currently, this species is classified as Near Threatened (NT) on the IUCN Red List and its numbers today are decreasing.

POPULATION THREATS

The major threat facing Silvery lutungs is the destruction of their habitat due to logging, the development of oil plantations and forest fires. These monkeys are also threatened by hunting for meat and by capture for the pet trade.

RED-FACED SPIDER MONKEY

The Red-faced spider monkey is a species of spider monkey that lives in South America. These monkeys have long, black hair and a red or pink face that is bare except for a few short, white hairs. Infants are born with dark faces, which lighten as they age. Red-faced spider monkeys have a prehensile (capable of grasping) tail and their fingers and limbs are long, agile and strong.

SCIENTIFIC CLASSIFICATION

Kingdom:	Animalia
Phylum:	Chordata
Class:	Mammalia
Order:	Primates
Family:	Atelidae
Genus:	Ateles
Species:	A. paniscus
Binomial name:	*Ateles paniscus*

Fact About Red-Faced Spider Monkey

- ✓ Group Name: Band, Troop, Barrel, Cartload, Tribe, Wilderness

- ✓ Lifestyle: Arboreal, Altricial, Zoochory, Scansorial, Terrestrial, Territorial

- ✓ Life Span: 34 - 46 Years

- ✓ Weight: 8.4-9 Kg

- ✓ Length: 55.2-55.7 Cm

DISTRIBUTION

- ✓ Continents: South America
- ✓ Countries: Brazil, Guyana, Suriname
- ✓ Regions: Roraima, Amapá, Pará
- ✓ Biomes: Tropical Moist Forests

Red-faced spider monkeys are found in northern South America. They live in northern Brazil, Suriname, Guyana, and French Guiana. Red-faced spider monkeys inhabit undisturbed primary rainforests.

HABITS AND LIFESTYLE

Red-faced spider monkeys are arboreal animals. Because of their ability to climb and jump, they tend to live in the upper layers of the trees and forage in the high canopy. These monkeys are social and associate with large groups of up to 30 individuals during the night, but choose to spend the days traveling, foraging, and resting in much smaller groups. At dusk, they recongregate using a greeting call to communicate. At night, they often sleep in large groups called bands. Bands typically consist of several females, with their respective young, along with a few males for protection.

Red-faced spider monkeys communicate with each other vocally by using grunts, screams, whistles, and barks, which warn others of predators or places where food can be found. Visual communication includes scratching their chests, shaking tree branches, throwing objects from trees, nodding their heads, and swinging their arms.

DIET AND NUTRITION

Red-faced spider monkeys are herbivores (frugivores, folivores). They feed primarily on a very wide variety of fruits, which comprise most of their diet. They also will eat young leaves and flowers, young seeds, floral buds, roots, bark and honey. Sometimes Red-faced spider monkeys may eat small insects such as termites and caterpillars.

MATING HABITS

- ✓ Mating Behavior: Polygynandry
- ✓ Gestation: 226-232 Days
- ✓ Baby Carrying: 4 Infants
- ✓ Independent Age: 15-18 Months
- ✓ Female Name: Female
- ✓ Male Name: Male

✓ Baby Name: Infant

Red-faced spider monkeys are polygynandrous (promiscuous), which means that both males and females have many partners during every breeding season. Females give birth to 4 infants every 3 to 4 years. The gestation period lasts around 226-232 days. During the first 2-3 months of life, infants cling to their mother's body and later from 6-9 months of age, young ride on their mother's backs. At 10 months infants begin to explore their environment independently, however, they still spend most of their time near their mother. At 15-18 months of age, infants begin to travel independently from their mother. Red-faced spider monkeys become reproductively mature at 4 to 5 years of age. Males often stay in their natal group but females leave to find potential mates and may return to their natal group to give birth to their offspring.

POPULATION THREATS

The main threats to Red-faced spider monkeys include hunting and habitat loss. These monkeys have a very slow reproductive rate giving birth to infants only every 3-4 years which affects the decline of their populations even more.

POPULATION NUMBER

The IUCN Red List and other sources don't provide the number of the Red-faced spider monkey total population size. Currently, this species is classified as Vulnerable (VU) on the IUCN Red List and its numbers today are decreasing.

ECOLOGICAL NICHE

Due to their frugivorous diet, these monkeys disperse seeds of various plants they consume. This way they highly benefit the local ecosystem.

JAVAN LANGUR

The East Javan langur, also known as the ebony lutung, Javan langur or Javan lutung, is an Old World monkey from the Colobinae subfamily. It is most commonly glossy black with a brownish tinge to its legs, sides, and "sideburns". It is found on the island of Java, as well as on several of the surrounding Indonesian islands. The Latin word auratus in its scientific name means "golden", and refers to a less common color variant. Note that the common name golden langur is used for a different species.

SCIENTIFIC CLASSIFICATION

Kingdom: Animalia

Phylum: Chordata

Class: Mammalia

Order: Primates

Family: Cercopithecidae

Genus: Trachypithecus

Species: T. auratus

Binomial name: *Trachypithecus auratus*

DIET AND NUTRITION

Mostly folivorous. Leaves, flowers, seeds of fruits, fruits, rarely insects and larvae.

Diet: Folivore, Frugivore, Herbivore

MATING HABITS

- ✓ Mating Behavior: Cooperative Breeder, Polygyny, Polygamy.

- ✓ Baby Carrying: 1

- ✓ Independent Age: 12 Months

FACT ABOUT JAVAN LANGUR

- ✓ Habitat: Dry Deciduous, Mangrove, Beach, And Freshwater Swamp Forests.

- ✓ Gestation: 7 Months, 1 Young.

- ✓ Social Structure: 5-21 Individuals (1 Or Rarely 2 Males And Many Females). Sometimes All Male Groups.

- ✓ Dimensions: Length   44-65cm

- ✓ Lifespan: ~20 Years

- ✓ Weight   7 Kg

✓ Length   44-65 Cm

✓ Lifestyle: Arboreal, Zoochory, Island Endemic, Scansorial, Terrestrial, Territorial.

POPULATION THREATS

Habitat loss and degradation due to expanding agriculture and human settlements, hunting for food or for the pet trade, fragmentation, and small isolated populations. IUCN Status: Vulnerable

DID YOU KNOW THAT

- ❑ All offspring are born with orange coat. Some specimens maintain this colouration when they mature, but this is more rare in the wild.

- ❑ They have large salivary glands which help them break down food easily.

- ❑ The name 'langur' means 'long tail' in Hindi. Their tail is longer than their body.

- ❑ Allomothering is common within the group.

- ❑ They have the important role of seed dispersal and reforestation in their ecosystem.

❑ Their only known predator is the human.

41

GOLDEN MONKEY

The Golden monkey is an insufficiently explored, but easily recognizable primate with a golden-orange patch on its upper flanks and back. This animal is an Old World monkey, endemic to Central Africa. In the past, the Golden monkey wasn't recognized as separate species, being considered a subspecies of the Blue monkey. In fact, these two monkeys are closely related and very similar. The ongoing divisions of forests has led to fragmentation of their range and Cercopithecus species have lived in isolated populations, where they have adapted to local environment. As a result, the Golden monkey has diverged from the Blue monkey. This endangered animal is one of the eight subspecies of the Blue monkey. Females of the golden monkey exhibit lighter coloration as well as less grizzled brown patches. However, there is very little information on the behavior and ecology of this species due to lack of observations.

SCIENTIFIC CLASSIFICATION

Kingdom: Animalia

Phylum: Chordata

Class: Mammalia

Order: Primates

Family: Cercopithecidae

Genus: Cercopithecus

Species:	C. kandti
Binomial name:	*Cercopithecus kandti*

FACT ABOUT GOLDEN MONKEY

- ✓ Life Span: 19 Years
- ✓ Weight: 3.5-7 Kg
- ✓ Length: 46-67
- ✓ Diet: Herbivore, Folivore, Frugivore
- ✓ Group Name: Troop, Barrel, Cartload, Tribe, Wilderness
- ✓ Lifestyle: Arboreal, Precocial, Terrestrial

DISTRIBUTION OF GOLDEN MONKEY

- ✓ Continents: Africa
- ✓ Subcontinents: Sub-Saharan Africa
- ✓ Countries: Angola, Burundi, Dr Congo, Ethiopia, Kenya, Malawi, Mozambique, Rwanda, Somalia, South Africa, Show More
- ✓ Biomes: Tropical Moist Forests, Tropical Savanna

The natural range of Golden monkey is limited to the Virunga volcanic mountains of Central Africa, where these animals occur in 4 national parks - Mgahinga (south-west Uganda), Volcanoes (north-west Rwanda), Virunga and Kahuzi-Biéga (eastern Democratic Republic of Congo). Ideal habitat for this species is highland forest with sufficient fruits and bamboo.

HABITS AND LIFESTYLE

Golden monkeys are highly social animals, forming groups of 30 - 80 individuals. Each of these units is dominated by a single mature male. The group size varies with elevation; as a general rule, groups at higher elevations are smaller. Females are constantly with the group to defend the territory, whereas males usually remain with the group temporarily, leaving it after a while. These monkeys are diurnal and arboreal. Their sleeping sites are located at tops of bamboo plants. When sleeping, Golden monkeys gather into smaller groups of 4 individuals on average. Feeding areas are usually found in close proximity to their sleeping sites, so these animals take daily trips to forage. Primary forms of communication, used by these primates, are visual expressions and various vocalizations. Some of these vocalizations are used by males during confrontations or when defending their territories. Females of this species use a wide range of calls to keep unity of the group as well as alert community members of potential threats. Meanwhile, sub-adults are known to accompany mobbing behavior with certain calls. Additionally, young individuals may display submissiveness through vocalizations.

DIET AND NUTRITION

Bamboo is the backbone of the golden monkey's diet. Essentially all parts of the plant are consumed. This species has also been known to feed on fresh fruit when available, and on flowers and shrubs. From time to time they will eat larvae. When they aren't eating bamboo, golden monkeys have been known to weave it together to make structures for sleeping.

The Golden monkey is herbivore (folivores and frugivore), it generally feeds upon bamboo leaves, bamboo branchlets, bamboo shoots, fruits, flowers, and shrubs, supplementing this diet with occasional invertebrates such as the pupae of lepidopterous larvae, found on leaves.

MATING HABITS

- ✓ Pregnancy Duration: 5 Months
- ✓ Baby Carrying: 1 Infant
- ✓ Independent Age: 2 Years
- ✓ Female Name: Female
- ✓ Male Name: Male
- ✓ Baby Name: Infant

Little is known about the mating system in Golden monkeys. However, as their groups consist of multiple females and only one male, it may mean that Golden monkeys may exhibit either polygynous or polygynandrous (promiscuous) mating systems. Although the male mates with all females of the group, mating is initiated by females. These primates are seasonal breeders. Gestation period lasts for 5 months, yielding one infant. Females give birth every two years. A newborn baby is well-developed. It comes with its total fur and open eyes. During the first few months, the baby is nursed by its mother. By the end of this period, the female gradually minimizes the nursing and eventually stops to produce a new young. Once becoming sexually mature, the baby will leave its natal group.

POPULATION THREATS

Most of threats to the population of this species are associated with human activity. Thus, the Golden monkeys suffer from habitat disturbance and are often caught in snares. These animals are also threatened by illegal destruction of their bamboo habitat.

POPULATION NUMBER

The IUCN Red List and other sources don't provide the number of the Golden monkeys' total population. However, this species' numbers are decreasing today, and the animal is classified as Endangered (EN) on the IUCN Red List.

WOLF'S MONA MONKEY

Wolf's mona monkey, also called Wolf's guenon, is a colourful Old World monkey in the family Cercopithecidae. It is found in central Africa, primarily between the Democratic Republic of the Congo and Uganda. It lives in primary and secondary lowland rainforest and swamp forest.

SCIENTIFIC CLASSIFICATION

Kingdom:	Animalia
Phylum:	Chordata
Class:	Mammalia
Order:	Primates
Family:	Cercopithecidae
Genus:	Cercopithecus
Species:	C. wolfi
Binomial name:	*Cercopithecus wolfi*

FACT ABOUT WOLF'S MONA MONKEY

- ✓ Weight: 2.4-4.2 Kg
- ✓ Length: 445-511 Mm

GEOGRAPHY

- ✓ Continents: Africa
- ✓ Countries: Dr Congo

✓ Biomes: Afro-tropical

HABITS AND LIFESTYLE

✓ Lifestyle: Arboreal, Zoochory,

Scansorial, Terrestrial,

Territorial.

DIET AND NUTRITION

✓ Diet Frugivore, Herbivore

MATING HABITS

✓ Mating Behavior: Polygyny, Polygamy

✓ Pregnancy Duration: 160 - 170 Days

✓ Baby Carrying: 1 - 2

✓ Independent Age: 180 Days

RED-SHANKED DOUC

The Red-shanked douc is a species of Old World monkey. They are the most colorful monkeys among all species of primates. They are considered "Queen of primates" thanks to their distinctive and unique appearance. Their forearms are white, upper legs black to grey and the lower legs are deep red while hands and feet are black. The monkey's yellow-orange face and ears are powdered with theatrical makeup, and the eyelids are dusted with a powder-blue eyeshadow. There is a slight difference in rump markings between genders: the male has round white spots above the triangle of white on its rump, while the female does not. Shortly, the douc's fur is a harmonious combination of the 5 colors: black, grey, white, brown-red and orange. Due to this fact, the species is also called the five-color douc. A baby douc has yellow-brown fur with black face.

SCIENTIFIC CLASSIFICATION

Kingdom: Animalia

Phylum: Chordata

Class: Mammalia

Order: Primates

Family: Cercopithecidae

Genus: Pygathrix

Species: P. nemaeus

Binomial name: *Pygathrix nemaeus*

FACTS ABOUT RED-SHANKED DOUC

- ✓ Life Span: 25 Years
- ✓ Weight: 8-11 Kg
- ✓ Length: 54.5-61 Cm
- ✓ Group Name: Troop, Barrel, Cartload, Tribe, Wilderness
- ✓ Lifestyle: Arboreal, Browsing, Precocial, Zoochory, Nomadic, Terrestrial.

DISTRIBUTION

- ✓ Continents: Asia
- ✓ Subcontinents: Southeast Asia
- ✓ Countries: Cambodia, Laos, Viet Nam
- ✓ Biomes: Tropical Moist Forests

Red-shanked doucs are found in southeast Asia. They are native to Indochina; Vietnam, Southern Laos and possibly Northeastern Cambodia. These monkeys live in a variety of habitats: from lowland to mountainous terrain, semi-deciduous, primary and secondary rainforests, in the mid to upper levels of the canopy.

HABITS AND LIFESTYLE

Red-shanked doucs are arboreal and diurnal monkeys that eat and sleep in the trees of the forest. They occasionally get on the ground to drink water or eat dirt that contains minerals. Like all monkeys, they are social animals that live in groups of 4-15, but may also agthr in groups of up to 50. A group usually consists of one or more males and approximately two females per male. Both males and females have their own hierarchies and males are dominant to females. Both males and females will eventually leave the group they were born into. When on the move, the group is led by adult males, with juvenile males bringing up the rear and the females and infants staying safe in the middle. These monkeys prefer moving high up in the canopy and are very agile. They frequently make breath-taking leaps of up to 6 meters (20 feet). When the group is untroubled, Red-shanked doucs move noisily from branch to branch through the forest, displaying their remarkable sense of balance. But when the group is disturbed, it can flee soundlessly through the trees, away from danger. If it is startled, it may give loud barks and rush around the trees slapping branches with their hands and feet. In contrast to their noisy travel, doucs spend most of their time quietly eating, digesting their bulky food, dozing and grooming each other's fur.

DIET AND NUTRITION

Red-shanked doucs are herbivores (folivores). They prefer to eat small, young and tender leaves, but will also eat fruit like figs, buds, petioles, flowers, bamboo shoots, and seeds. DIET Herbivore, Folivore.

MATING HABITS

- ✓ Mating Behavior: Polygyny
- ✓ Reproduction Season: August-December
- ✓ Gestation Period: 165-190 Days
- ✓ Baby Carrying: 1 Infant
- ✓ Female Name: Female
- ✓ Male Name: Male
- ✓ Baby Name: Infant

Red-shanked doucs are polygynous which means that males mate with more than one female during the breeding season. Before mating, both genders attract each other with signals that inckude the jaw forward, eyebrows raised and then lowered, and a head-shake. The female makes the first move, lying face-down on a branch, eyeing her chosen mate by looking over her shoulder. The male returns with a stare. Mating takes place from August to December. The pregnancy lasts between 165-190 days, resulting in the birth of a single baby just before fruiting season of some favorite foods. Twins are very rare. The young are born with their eyes wide open and they cling to their mothers instinctively. In captivity, other group members may look after an infant, and other females may even suckle it. In one study, an orphaned infant was fed by two females in the group and also cared for by a male. Females in this species reach reproductive maturity at about 4 years, while the males become mature at 4-5 years.

POPULATION THREATS

The major threat to this species at presnt is hunting, most often for subsistence use and traditional medicine. Local people often hunt Red-shanked doucs for food, pets or making glue.

For the population in Son Tra (Vietnam), habitat loss due to development plan poses the biggest risk to them.

POPULATION NUMBER

The IUCN Red List and other sources don't provide the number of the Red-shanked douc total population size. According to Wikipedia in Son Tra (Vietnam), the douc population is around 1300 individuals. Currently, this species is classified as Endangered (EN) on the IUCN Red List and its numbers today are decreasing.

ECOLOGICAL NICHE

As herbivorous animals, Red-shanked doucs serve as plant dispersers of their range.

OLIVE BABOON OR DOG-FACED BABOON

This baboon is a type of old-world monkey (a monkey species from the Eastern Hemisphere) that roams across various habitats of Africa. They have numerous adaptations to help them survive and thrive in different environmental conditions. In this article, you will learn some interesting facts about the physical and behavioral characteristics, including reproduction, lifespan, and identification, of the olive baboon.

SCIENTIFIC CLASSIFICATION

Kingdom:	Animalia
Phylum:	Chordata
Class:	Mammalia
Order:	Primates
Family:	Cercopithecidae
Genus:	Papio
Species:	P. anubis
Binomial name:	*Papio anubis*

OLIVE BABOON FACTS

- ✓ Prey: Rodents, Birds, Insects, Fruits, Roots, Seeds, Leaves, Bark, Flowers.

- ✓ Name Of Young: Infant

- ✓ Biggest Threat: Hunting And Habitat Loss

- ✓ Gestation Period: 180 Days

- ✓ Litter Size: One

- ✓ Habitat: Savannahs, Grasslands, Deserts, And Rainforests

- ✓ Predators: Leopards, Crocodiles, Raptors, Hyenas, Wild Dogs, Chimpanzees.

- ✓ Diet: Omnivore

- ✓ Type: Primate

- ✓ Common Name: Olive Baboon

- ✓ Number Of Species: 1

- ✓ Location: Central Africa

- ✓ Other Name: Anubis Baboon

Fun Fact

❑ Olive Baboons Will Sometimes Form Strong Friendships With Each Other

Most Distinctive Feature

❑ The Long Canines On The Male

Olive Baboon Physical Characteristics

✓ Color: Grey, Grey-Brown

✓ Skin Type: Fur

✓ Lifespan: 25 Years

✓ Weight: 30-55 Pounds

✓ Height: Two Feet

✓ Length: 19-30 Inches

✓ Age Of Sexual Maturity: 25 Years

FIVE INCREDIBLE OLIVE BABOON FACTS!

❑ The olive baboon has the ability to mate and produce viable offspring with the yellow baboon and sometimes even the Guinea baboon.

❑ One of the baboon's most important

adaptations is the ability to extract nutrients from just about any source. This helps the baboon survive even in dry climates.

❑ A group of 60 olive baboons escaped from a Spanish safari park in 1972 and established a free population. They were eventually recaptured and then sent to various zoos.

❑ Baboons have cheek pouches to store food for later.

❑ Olive baboons apparently play an important ecological role by dispersing undigested seeds throughout the environment.

BEHAVIOR

As a primate, the olive baboon has one of the most complicated social systems in the entire animal kingdom. The social structure, also known as the troop, consists of several males and females living together at once. Featuring up to 150 members, troops are absolutely vital for the survival of the baboon, because members travel, forage, groom, sleep together, and protect each other from dangerous predators. The troop is composed of separate male and female dominance hierarchies based on strength and seniority. Higher ranked members will have access to more food and mates. However, these hierarchies may change frequently, and relationships and friendships can be established between members of different ranks.

HABITAT

The olive baboon can be found in savannah, grasslands, deserts, and rainforests throughout central sub-Saharan Africa, from the Atlantic coast to the horn of Africa, which encompasses some 25 countries in total. There are also isolated populations within the Saharan Desert. Unlike most monkey species, baboons live primarily on the ground, but they are capable climbers as well.

REPRODUCTION AND LIFE CYCLE

The olive baboon follows a promiscuous mating strategy. While larger, stronger, and younger males tend to dominate access to mates, two males will sometimes form alliances with each other (especially between older males who are well-acquainted) to wrest away access from a third more dominant male. Sometimes a softer approach is required, however. Males will attempt to forge a bond with females by grooming, sharing food, and defending her from other baboons. Females appear to show a preference for mating with male friends.

Mating can occur at any time throughout the year. Healthy females who have the most access to food (this is usually the highest ranked females) can breed annually; otherwise, they will breed once every 12 to 34 months. Because lactation causes a significant fall in the mother's weight, it requires a significant amount of time to recover from. After mating, the female will give birth to a single offspring about half a year later.

Born with black coat colors and pink skin, the baby is completely dependent on the mother. She provides much of the nursing, grooming, and playtime, whereas the father plays a minimal role in parental duties. The fur will grow the olive gray colors at around the first year of age, but it takes more than 400 days before the baby is completely weaned off its mother's milk and begins eating solid food.

The sexual maturity of the baboon is heavily dependent on its nutritional intake. If well-fed, it can reach full sexual maturity in as little as five or six years. Males will undergo several important changes in physical characteristics, including muscle growth, deeper voices, the eruption of the teeth, and the development of the mane. Before that point, identification of the sexes is very difficult. The lifespan of this species has never been accurately recorded, but based on observation of closely related baboons, it can probably live an average of 25 years.

POPULATION

The olive baboon is considered to be a species of least concern by the IUCN Red List. Scientists do not have enough facts about their populations to determine or estimate their numbers.

PREDATORS AND THREATS

Olive baboons face a few threats from humans. They are sometimes shot, trapped, and poisoned in retaliation for consuming crops or livestock. They are also at risk of habitat loss from encroaching farms. However, this has not appeared to impact their population seriously enough to warrant a downgrade in their conservation status. Local farmers can sometimes deter baboons with domestic dogs and other methods.

LION TAILED MACAQUE

The magnificent Lion-tailed macaque is an Old World monkey, named due to its lion-like, long, thin and tufted tail. This adorable primate is unfortunately among most endangered of the macaques around the globe. In the meantime, this animal is one of the smallest macaque species in the world. The Lion-tailed macaque is endemic and native exclusively to Western Ghats (India). It's a living proof of the amazing diversity of its mountain rainforest habitat. As a result of its shy and solitary nature, this animal doesn't tend to venture from its usual range, travelling only within its rainforest habitat.

SCIENTIFIC CLASSIFICATION

Kingdom: Animalia

Phylum: Chordata

Class: Mammalia

Order: Primates

Family: Cercopithecidae

Genus: Macaca

Species: M. silenus

Binomial name   *Macaca silenus*

FACT ABOUT LION TAILED MACAQUE

- ✓ Population Size: Below 4,000
- ✓ Life Span: 20-38 Yrs
- ✓ Weight: 3-10 Kg
- ✓ Length: 40-61 Cm
- ✓ Group Name: Troop, Barrel, Cartload, Tribe, Wilderness
- ✓ Lifestyle: Arboreal, Altricial, Zoochory, Terrestrial, Territorial.

DISTRIBUTION

- ✓ Continents: Asia
- ✓ Subcontinents: South Asia
- ✓ Countries: India
- ✓ Regions: Karnataka, Kerala, Tamil Nadu
- ✓ Biomes: Tropical Moist Forests

The natural range of this species is restricted to the Western Ghats Mountains, located in southwestern part of India. Preferred habitat of the Lion-tailed macaques is broad leaf trees, growing in monsoon forests as well as evergreen and semi-evergreen rainforests.

HABITS AND LIFESTYLE

These highly social primates are known to form family units of up to 34 individuals with an average of 10 - 20. Each group consists of a single dominant male and, sometimes, 1 - 2 additional adult males. The dominant male of the group controls breeding. Members of these family units not only travel collectively, but also sleep huddling together. As arboreal and diurnal creatures, they sleep at night in trees (typically, high in the canopy of rainforest). These macaques are territorial and very communicative animals. One of the distinguishing features of this species is that males define boundaries of their home ranges by calls. Dominant males of different groups emit loud, human-like 'whoops', after which one of the troops leaves the territory. Overall, their communication system contains as many as 17 vocalizations. Along with calls, the Lion-tailed macaques also use body language. For example, they greet each other by smacking their lips, whereas yawning with a grimace is a display of dominance or threat.

DIET AND NUTRITION

As omnivorous animals, Lion-tailed macaques feed upon a wide variety of food, although fruits form the major part of their diet. Suitable foods include leaves, stems, flowers, buds, fungi as well as meat such as insects, lizards, tree frogs and various small mammals.DIET Omnivore

MATING HABITS

- ✓ Mating Behavior: Polygyny
- ✓ Reproduction Season: Year-Round
- ✓ Pregnancy Duration: 6 Months
- ✓ Baby Carrying: 1 Infant
- ✓ Independent Age: 1 Year
- ✓ Female Name: Female
- ✓ Male Name: Male
- ✓ Baby Name: Infant

Lion-tailed macaques are polygynous, which

means that one male gets an exclusive right to mating with multiple females. Lion-tailed macaques breed year-round. However, birth rate usually increases during the wet season, when there is sufficient amount of food. Gestation period lasts for about 6 months, yielding a single infant, which is helpless and completely depends on its mother. The newborn baby is carried on its mother's abdomen. The infant is cared by its mother for a long period of time as it grows and learns various skills. Nursing period lasts for about one year. Soon the young macaques reach adolescence, after which males disperse to join nomadic all-male units, until they form and maintain their own harems. Meanwhile, females usually continue living with their natal group. The age of sexual maturity is 5 years old in females and 8 years old in males.

POPULATION THREATS

The biggest threat to the overall population of this species is the destruction of their rainforest habitat. In fact, these primates have lost as much as 99% of their original range as a result of large-scale deforestation for timber, agriculture and development. Lion-tailed macaques live in isolated populations, which are unable to interbreed.

Hence, these fragmented populations currently face sharp decline. Additionally, the Lion-tailed macaques are frequently killed because of being mistaken for Nilgiri langurs, which are commonly hunted for their meat that is falsely believed to have medicinal properties. Other notable threats include persecution as pest species due to raiding crops.

POPULATION NUMBER

According to the IUCN Red List, the total population of Lion-tailed macaques is under 4,000 individuals, including less than 2,500 mature individuals. Specific populations have been estimated in the following areas: The forests of Kerala – up to 1,216 adult macaques; Tamil Nadu (the Anaimalai Hills) - about 500 individuals. Overall, the population number of Lion-tailed macaques is decreasing today, and the animals are classified as Endangered (EN) on the IUCN Red List.

ECOLOGICAL NICHE

Lion-tailed macaques play some role in the ecosystem they live, as they disperse seeds of fruits and plants they consume. They may also affect predator populations, as items of prey.

LANGUR MONKEY

75

Langur, general name given to numerous species of Asian monkeys belonging to the subfamily Colobinae. The term is often restricted to nearly two dozen species of leaf monkeys but is also applied to various other members of the subfamily.

SCIENTIFIC CLASSIFICATION

Kingdom: Animalia

Phylum: Chordata

Class: Mammalia

Order: Primates

Family: Cercopithecidae

Subfamily: Colobinae

Tribe: Presbytini

Genus: Semnopithecus

Species: S. Schistaceus

Binomial name: Semnopithecus entellus

FACT ABOUT LANGUR MONKEY

- ✓ Weight: 9.9 -13 Kg

- ✓ Length: 58.5 -64 Cm

The northern plains gray langur, also known as the sacred langur, Bengal sacred langur and Hanuman langur, is a species of primate in the family Cercopithecidae.

DISTRIBUTION

- ✓ Continents: Asia
- ✓ Countries: India
- ✓ Introduced Countries: Bangladesh
- ✓ Regions: Bihar, Orissa, West Bengal, Andhra Pradesh, Chattisgarh, Jharkand, Maharashtra.

HABITS AND LIFESTYLE

- ✓ Lifestyle: Arboreal, Zoochory, Scansorial, Terrestrial, Territorial.
- ✓ Seasonal Behavior: Aestivation and Not A Migrant

DIET AND NUTRITION

✓ Diet: Folivore, Herbivore.

MATING HABITS

✓ Mating Behavior: Polygynandry,

                              Polygamy, Polygyny.

✓ Pregnancy Duration: 200 - 212 Days

✓ Baby Carrying: 1 - 2

✓ Independent Age: 1 - 2 Years

APES

Apes are primates. Primates are mammals that share the following characteristics:

- ❑ Hair instead of fur

- ❑ Fingernails instead of claws

- ❑ Opposable thumbs

- ❑ Higher brain-to-body size ratio, high level of intelligence

- ❑ Prehensility (ability to grasp with fingers and/or toes)

- ❑ Padded digits with fingerprints

- ❑ Binocular vision i.e. both eyes focus on one object (depth perception)

- ❑ Reduced olfactory sense and dependent on vision more than smell

People often confuse apes and monkeys. Although there are a number of differences between apes and monkeys which are:

- ❖ Apes have a longer lifespan,

- ❖ Larger body size,

- ❖ Larger brain-to-body size ratio, and higher intelligence

- ❖ The main difference is that monkeys have tails and apes do not have tails.

The difference between great apes and lesser apes is general size. There are two types of lesser apes:

i.   Gibbons (SouthEastern Asia) and

ii.   Siamangs (SouthEastern Asia).

There are four types of great apes:

i.   Gorillas (Africa),

ii.   Bonobos (Africa),

iii.   Orangutans (SouthEastern Asia), and

iv.   Chimpanzees (Africa).

They are all explained below with illustrations.

GO RI LLA
CHIM PAN ZEE
ORA NGU TAN

GORILLA

The Western gorilla is a massive primate species with a short muzzle, proportionately large hands and the projecting brow ridge. They lack tails, having small ears and eyes, large nostrils and jet black skin. They have quite a large thumb and nails on all digits. They have large muscles on their jaws as well as strong, broad teeth. The whole body, with the exception of the face, ears, hands, and feet, is covered with dark tough fur. The fur of Western gorillas is brown to grey in color. Older male gorillas are called "silverbacks" due to the hair on their back and rump, which is originally grey, loosing with age.

SCIENTIFIC CLASSIFICATION

Kingdom: Animalia

Phylum: Chordata

Class: Mammalia

Order: Primates

Family: Hominidae

Subfamily: Homininae

Tribe: Gorillini

Genus: Gorilla

Species:	G. gorilla
Binomial name:	*Gorilla gorilla*

FACT ABOUT GORILLA

- ✓ Life Span: 35-50 Yrs
- ✓ Top Speed: 40 Km/H
- ✓ Weight: 80-157 Kg
- ✓ Height: 135-155 Cm
- ✓ Wingspan: Males 175Cm; Females 125Cm
- ✓ Group Name: Band, Troop, Whoop
- ✓ Lifestyle: Terrestrial, Arboreal, Altricial, Browsing

DISTRIBUTION

- ✓ Continents: Africa
- ✓ Subcontinents: Sub-Saharan Africa
- ✓ Countries: Angola, Cameroon, Central African Republic, Congo, Equatorial Guinea, Gabon, Nigeria.
- ✓ Biomes: Tropical Moist Forests

The animals occur in tropical jungles, forests, lowland swamps and secondary forests of West Central Africa.

HABITS AND LIFESTYLE

These primates are highly social animals, gathering in groups of 5-15 individuals. A group usually consists of females with their young and one dominant male. They get around by walking on their four limbs. Western gorillas are active by day. They construct day and night nests where they rest and sleep. Their nests are soft cushions, built on the ground or in trees, out of branches and leaves. Lightweight gorillas tend to hang out of tree branches, using their arms. Normally, these animals are quite peaceful, friendly and shy. However, they emit loud growling sounds and can be extremely dangerous, when threatened or attacked. In order to scare away intruders or demonstrate their strength, male gorillas stand straight, beating their chests with their fists. Nevertheless, they don't tend to hit the opponent, instead preferring to retreat and then charge again.

DIET AND NUTRITION

These gorillas are herbivorous (folivorous) animals. Their diet primarily consists of juicy stemmed plants, complemented by berries, ferns, bark and leaves. Diet is Herbivore, Folivore

MATING HABITS

- ✓ Mating Behavior: Polygyny
- ✓ Reproduction Season: Year-Round
- ✓ Gestation Period: 251-289 Days
- ✓ Baby Carrying: 1 Infant
- ✓ Independent Age: 3 Years
- ✓ Female Name: Female
- ✓ Male Name: Male
- ✓ Baby Name: Infant

They have polygynous mating system with the only dominant male, mating with females of the group. They breed all year round. Gestation period lasts 251-289 days, yielding a single baby, rarely - twins. The infant is kept belly-to-belly to its mother, until the age of 2 month, when the baby is mature and strong enough to be able to cling onto the mother's fur. Weaning takes place at the age of 3 years. Male gorillas are sexually mature at 8-9 years old, while females, a bit earlier - at the age of 7-8 years.

POPULATION THREATS

These animals are primarily threatened by human activities. For over a century, Western gorillas have suffered from degradation of their tropical rainforest habitat. They have been persecuted, hunted for meat and big games and captured for commercial trade. On the other hand, excessive collection by zoos and research institutions has brought to sharp decline of their population, making the animal an endangered species. Presently, one of the most notable threats to this species is Ebola virus: despite the conservation status, outbreaks of this virus are still a serious concern for Western gorillas' population.

POPULATION NUMBER

The overall number of their population is presently unknown, but decreasing. On the IUCN Red List, the Western gorilla is mentioned as Critically Endangered (CR) species.

ECOLOGICAL NICHE

Western gorillas are an important link in the ecosystem of their habitat. They are key seed dispersers of tropical rainforests, creating suitable places for the seeds to grow and thus sustaining a number of plant species. By doing this, they benefit many other animals of the area and even help sustain the habitat of humans, who live in and around the forests.

Gorilla is the world largest primate living on Earth

CHIMPANZEE

CHIMPANZEE CLASSIFICATION AND EVOLUTION

The Chimpanzee is a species of ape that is natively found in a variety of different habitats in western and central Africa. Closely related to other great apes including Orangutans and Gorillas, the Chimpanzee is an animal that is also very closely related to Humans as we share 98% of the same DNA. They are thought to be the most intelligent animals on the planet after people and are not only known to show emotion but they are also great problem-solvers and are even known to not just use, but also make tools to help them to survive more successfully in their surroundings. There are two different species of Chimpanzee which are the Common Chimpanzee and the smaller Bonobo (also known as the Pygmy Chimpanzee) which has a limited distribution south of the Congo River. However, despite being highly adaptable and intelligent creatures, Chimpanzees are severely threatened in their natural habitats today, mainly due to hunting for bushmeat and deforestation.

SCIENTIFIC CLASSIFICATION

Kingdom:	Animalia
Phylum:	Chordata
Class:	Mammalia
Order:	Primates
Family:	Hominidae
Subfamily:	Homininae
Tribe:	Hominini
Genus:	Pan
Species:	P. troglodytes
Binomial name:	*Pan troglodytes*

FACT ABOUT CHIMPANZEE

- ✓ Conservation Status: Endangered
- ✓ Locations: Africa
- ✓ Prey: Fruits, Seeds, Insects
- ✓ Name Of Young: Infant
- ✓ Group Behavior: Group

- ✓ Population Size: 100,000 - 200,000

- ✓ Biggest Threat: Habitat loss

- ✓ Other Name: Common Chimpanzee

- ✓ Gestation Period: 8 months

- ✓ Habitat: Tropical forest and woody savanna

- ✓ Predators: Leopards, Snakes, Humans

- ✓ Diet: Omnivore

- ✓ Average Litter Size: **1**

- ✓ Lifestyle: Diurnal

- ✓ Common Name: Chimpanzee

- ✓ Number Of Species: **2**

- ✓ Location: Western and Central Africa

- ✓ Group: Mammal

FUN FACT

- ▪ Has 32 teeth including fang-like canines!

MOST DISTINCTIVE FEATURE

- Dexterous hands and feet and complex communication.

CHIMPANZEE PHYSICAL CHARACTERISTICS

- ✓ Colour: Brown, Black

- ✓ Skin Type: Hair

- ✓ Top Speed: 25 mph

- ✓ Lifespan: 50 - 60 years

- ✓ Weight: 26kg - 70kg (57lbs - 154lbs)

- ✓ Height: 1m - 1.7m (3.25ft - 5.5ft)

- ✓ Age of Sexual Maturity: 13 - 16 years

- ✓ Age of Weaning: 5 - 6 years

CHIMPANZEE ANATOMY AND APPEARANCE

Chimpanzees are large primates that have long yet sparse black hairs covering their bodies with the exception of their face, palms and the soles of their feet. Their hair not only allows them to remain warm in areas at higher altitudes but it also provides their skin with some protection from the sun. The hairless parts of their bodies are light to dark brown in colour depending on the age of the individual (their skin darkens as they mature). They have large ears that give them excellent hearing and a heavy brow-ridge over their eyes. Like other great apes, Chimpanzees are animals that have good sight and are able to see in colour, while their forward facing eyes allow them to focus on a single object clearly. They have long fingers and an opposable big toe that helps them to grip onto things, with their arms also being longer than their legs which enables them to move around on all fours which is known as knuckle-walking. Chimpanzees have 32 teeth which are very similar to those of Humans to help them to not just grind up plant matter but their longer canines also help to bite into flesh.

CHIMPANZEE DISTRIBUTION AND HABITAT

Chimpanzees are found throughout 21 different countries in western and central Africa where they are known to inhabit a variety of different regions from the tropical, humid rainforests to the dryer and more arid regions of the savanna and open woodlands. They are excellent climbers and rely heavily on the surrounding trees not just for protection from predators but also to find food and places to nest during the night. Chimpanzees have been severely affected by the loss of much of their natural habitat as forests are cleared to make way for agriculture or to cut down the trees as tropical timber. With groups being pushed into smaller and smaller ranges the competition for food and nesting sites increases and conflict can occur both between different groups and amongst individuals who reside in the same community.

CHIMPANZEE BEHAVIOUR AND LIFESTYLE

Chimpanzees are highly sociable animals that spend the daylight hours feeding, playing and grooming with other members of the group. Groups (also known as communities) can range in size from 15 to 120 individuals depending on the habitat and the amount of food available. They are highly territorial and do not tolerate outsiders in their midst, often killing an individual that is from another group. Chimpanzee groups have incredibly complex social structures with the dominant males not necessarily being the strongest individuals but more the ones that can rally together the most supporters. Chimpanzees make nests in the trees at night by folding over branches to provide them with a safe platform on which to sleep, with a new nest being constructed every day. Although they spend a lot of time both sleeping and eating in the trees and do move about by swinging from branch to branch, most travel is done using a network of paths on the ground using their knuckles to balance on.

CHIMPANZEE REPRODUCTION AND LIFE CYCLES

Although bonds within the group can last for many years, there are no long-term bonds between males and females as far as reproduction is concerned. Female Chimpanzees can give birth at any time of year to a single infant that is born after a gestation period that lasts for around eight months. After birth, the infant clings onto its mother's fur and will remain with her solidly for the first few years when the young begin to get more adventurous and starts to explore their surroundings increasingly more on their own. Young Chimpanzees learn the skills they need to survive by watching their mother including what to eat, how to make tools and nest building, along with playing with other young individuals to practise both their grooming and wrestling skills. Females are thought to be able to reproduce at 13 years of age where males seem to develop slightly later and breed when they are about 16 years old.

CHIMPANZEE DIET AND PREY

The Chimpanzee is an omnivorous animal that eats hundreds of different types of food. The bulk of their diet is comprised of seasonal fruits, seeds and flowers that are picked from the trees, along with insects such as ants and termites that are extracted from their nests using a stick. However, they are known to eat larger prey too and when working together, sub-groups are able to kill monkeys and birds and have even been known to successfully hunt small antelope. Chimpanzees are the only animals (apart from Orang-Utans and Humans) that don't just use tools but also make them. They are known to strip the leaves and twigs off branches which are then inserted into a termite mound, where the termites crawl onto the branch and the Chimpanzee then licks them off. They are also known to use stones as hammers to open nuts and have even been known to use chewed leaves as a sponge to soak up water, which is then drunk from the leaf.

CHIMPANZEE PREDATORS AND THREATS

Due to the fact that they spend so much time in the trees, Chimpanzees are not at great risk from many of the large predators that are found on the ground. There are however, animals that can live both on the ground and in the trees with Leopards being one of the biggest natural threats to these animals. Chimpanzees are also preyed upon by large species of snake and can be killed by other primates (including other Chimpanzees). Infants are at greater risk than their parents as they have even been known to be captured and eaten by Baboons that share their ranges. The biggest threat to Chimpanzees though is people that have not only hunted them for their meat but have also wiped out vast areas of their natural habitats, meaning fewer trees to eat and rest in.

CHIMPANZEE INTERESTING FACTS AND FEATURES

Chimpanzees are highly sociable and spend much time every day grooming one-another. Not only does this keep them clean and free from parasites but it is also thought to be relaxing for them and strengthens social bonds within the group. Chimpanzees are known to make 30 distinct calls with which they communicate with other members of the group, including the pant-hoot. This series of shrieks and roars is the most common noise for an adult Chimpanzee to make and can be heard up to 2km away. Although they do make a variety of different sounds, most communication is through facial expression. They have very flexible lips which are curled apart to produce a "smile" that actually signifies fear when they are either angry or feel threatened. Chimpanzees are known to be one of the world's most intelligent animal species and cannot only remember things but are also able to recognise themselves in a mirror.

CHIMPANZEE RELATIONSHIP WITH

HUMANS

Chimpanzees and Humans are thought to share a common ancestor that lived around 8 million years ago but Chimpanzees have been severely affected by their closest relatives. People have hunted and killed Chimpanzees for bushmeat which still continues today (despite being prohibited), with some populations having also been devastated as they inhabit regions which have been in long periods of civil war. However, it is the loss of their natural habitats which is having the worst affect on Chimpanzees as they need the trees around them to survive. Despite the lack of care for them in the wild, the human-like nature of Chimpanzees has fascinated people for years both in science and in zoos where there are always people crowding around, enjoying watching them interact.

ORANGUTAN

The name orangutan means "man of the forest" in the Malay language. In the lowland forests in which they reside, orangutans live solitary existences. They feast on wild fruits like lychees, mangosteens, and figs, and slurp water from holes in trees. They make nests in trees of vegetation to sleep at night and rest during the day. Adult male orangutans can weigh up to 200 pounds. Flanged males have prominent cheek pads called flanges and a throat sac used to make loud verbalizations called long calls. An unflanged male looks like an adult female. In a biological phenomenon unique among primates, an unflanged male can change to a flanged male for reasons that are not yet fully understood.

SCIENTIFIC CLASSIFICATION

Kingdom:	Animalia
Phylum:	Chordata
Class:	Mammalia
Order:	Primates
Family:	Hominidae
Subfamily:	Ponginae
Genus:	Pongo
Species:	P. pygmaeus

Binomial Name: *Pongo pygmaeus*

FACT ABOUT ORANGUTAN

- ✓ Common Name: Orangutans

- ✓ Type: Mammals

- ✓ Diet: Omnivore

- ✓ Average Life Span: 30-40 Years

- ✓ Size: Standing Height: 4 - 5 Feet

- ✓ Weight: 73-180Ib

SIZE

Orangutans have an enormous arm span. A male may stretch his arms some 7 feet from fingertip to fingertip—a reach considerably longer than his standing height of about 5 feet. When orangutans do stand, their hands nearly touch the ground.

LIFE IN THE TREES

Orangutans' arms are well suited to their lifestyle because they spend much of their time (some 90 percent) in the trees of their tropical rain forest home. They even sleep aloft in nests of leafy branches. They use large leaves as umbrellas and shelters to protect themselves from the common rains.

DIET AND NUTRITION

These cerebral primates forage for food during daylight hours. Most of their diet consists of fruit and leaves gathered from rain forest trees. They also eat bark, insects and, on rare occasions, meat.

SOLITARY BEHAVIOR

Orangutans are more solitary than other apes. Males are loners. As they move through the forest they make plenty of rumbling, howling calls to ensure that they stay out of each other's way. The "long call" can be heard 1.2 miles away.

REPRODUCTION

Mothers and their young, however, share a strong bond. Infants will stay with their mothers for some six or seven years until they develop the skills to survive on their own. Female orangutans give birth only once every eight years—the longest time period of any animal. The animals are long-lived and have survived as long as 60 years in captivity.

THREATS TO SURVIVAL

Because orangutans live in only a few places, and because they are so dependent upon trees, they are particularly susceptible to logging in these areas. Unfortunately, deforestation and other human activities, such as hunting, have placed the orangutan in danger of extinction.

Feeding Regime for The Animals in Primate Section in Kano Zoological Garden

Using Kano zoological garden in Northwestern Nigeria as a case study. The animals in primate section present in the aforementioned life collection was thoroughly observed by myself during my study skill carried out in the life collection.

All the animals in this section are fed twice a day; in the morning they took their breakfast with series of fruits such as oranges, cucumber, garden eggs, bananas and sweet potatoes, these fruits are served to them in their inner room or rest room. In the afternoon cooked rice and beans are been served to them as lunch in their rest room. These routine is repeated on a daily basis, and it is accompanied with clean water. The proportion of food nutrient serve to them as breakfast and as lunch respectively are breakdown on the table below;

	Morning (Breakfast)		Afternoon (Lunch)		
Fruit	Amount of nutrients served		Rice and Beans	Amount of nutrients served	
	Mineral	Vitamin		Mineral	Vitamin
	5.4g	0.6g		21g	28g

Feeding Table

REFERENCE

Aerts, R. (2019). Forest and woodland vegetation in the highlands of Dogu'a Tembien. In: Nyssen J., Jacob, M., Frankl, A. (Eds.). Geo-trekking in Ethiopia's Tropical Mountains - The Dogu'a Tembien District. SpringerNature. ISBN 978-3-030-04954-6. Retrieved 18 June 2019.

Groves, C. P. (2005). "Order Primates". In Wilson, D. E.; Reeder, D. M (eds.). Mammal Species of the World: A Taxonomic and Geographic Reference (3rd ed.). Johns Hopkins University Press. p. 166. ISBN 978-0-8018-8221-0. OCLC 62265494.

Shefferly, N. (2004). "Papio anubis". Animal Diversity Web. Retrieved 2007-01-27.

Wallis, J. (2020). "Monkey". IUCN Red List of Threatened Species. 2020: e.T40647A17953200. doi:10.2305/IUCN.UK.2020-2.RLTS.T40647A17953200.en. Retrieved 19 November 2021.

https://a-z-animals.com/animals/chimpanzee/

Orangutan Vs Gorilla

Chimpanzee Vs Gorilla

THE BOOK OF CARNIVORES